my dog has flies

poetry for hawai'i's kids

Poems by Sue Cowing
Illustrations by Jon J. Murakami

BEACHHOUSE
PUBLISHING, LLC

ISBN 1-933067-11-X
Library of Congress Catalog Card Number: 2005929118

First Printing, October 2005
1 2 3 4 5 6 7 8 9

BeachHouse Publishing, LLC
PO Box 2926
'Ewa Beach, Hawai'i 96706
Email: info@beachhousepublishing.com
www.beachhousepublishing.com

Printed in Korea

Acknowledgments

Boundless thanks to Jane Gillespie, of BeachHouse, for imagining and shepherding this book, and to the many readers/listeners who helped shape the poems: Shan Correa, Marion Coste, Ced Cowing, Ellie Crowe, Cammy Doi, Vicky Dworkin, Norma Gorst, Harry Kiefer, Seth Kiefer, Daya McCutcheon, Eric McCutcheon, Susan Morrison, Nancy Mower, Lyz Soto, Lynne Wikoff, Tammy Yee-Custodio, and especially Jim Rumford, peerless reader.

—S.C.

THE EMPTY LOT

Come with us to our favorite spot.
Some people call it the empty lot
'cause it doesn't have buildings or hot concrete
like every place else along this street.

Bring your dog along—leave his leash behind.
He can bark and chase mongoose. No one will mind.
He'll love the grass. It's three feet tall!
It looks like it's never been mowed at all.

Let's lie down flat in the grass and pretend
the whole town's a meadow that doesn't end.
Out here with the wind blowing through our hair
we can think anything. We can be anywhere.

We can float on the ocean and gaze at the sky
(that's surf you hear, not cars going by),
or imagine we're hang-gliding off a cliff.
It's a perfect place to ask "What if. . .?"

What if the zoo animals all ran loose?
What if a kid could speak mongoose
or glide like a ray or play dolphin games?
What if things all had different names?
What if nobody ever lied?
What if nobody ever died?

There are things to think that can only be thought
In what some people call an empty lot.

LION DANCER

Ever since Kevin was almost three
he's known for sure what he wanted to be:
a dancing lion in Chinatown
who rears up and swallows the red money down
and flutters his lashes and shakes his fur
to the clang of gongs in the smoky blur
from fireworks popping around his feet
as he prowls down Maunakea Street.

He always pictured himself as the head,
but he wound up being the tail instead
of the smallest lion owned by his group.
The whole time he's dancing, he has to stoop
and follow Keoki wherever he goes
(and jump to the side to protect his toes).
Though he hears people shouting, *Kung Hee Fat Choy!*,
Kevin's missing the fun. He's the back-up boy.

He sees mostly feet. When they go round a bend,
he has to watch out for Keoki's rear end.
Kevin knows he is lucky and shouldn't grumble.
They say it's a good thing in life to be humble.
But shouldn't Keoki be learning that too,
instead of hogging the lion's-head view?

DARIN'S PET

Every kid begs to have a pet,
but Darin came up with the best pet yet.
It can fit in his pocket, it's very small,
and it doesn't eat store-bought food at all.
It doesn't need kibbles or ground-up beef,
it makes its poop on a throw-away leaf,
and Darin can watch it crouch and leap
from hand to hand. It's a pet to keep!

So why do his parents grind their gears
and cry *No! No! No!* and cover their ears?
It's not like he's asking for a dog—
all he wants is this tiny frog
who sits in his hand and calls cheerfully,
coqui! coqui! coqui! coqui!

PET EXCHANGE

I had a pet duck I raised from an egg.
After feeding, he rubbed his beak on my leg.
I made him a pool so he could swim.
He loved me, I know, and I loved him.

Today when I put him back in his pen,
in one quick streak a mongoose got in,
but quicker than that my duck got out.
I shut the door of his pen with a shout.
He left one tail feather floating behind him.
I ran from the yard, but I couldn't find him.

The mongoose is still in the pen. Just my luck:
my friendly and shiny green mandarin duck
is out in the countryside running loose,
and here I am with a pet mongoose.

BULBUL OR MYNAH?

One bird at a time, you really can't tell
The bulbul's song from the mynah's well.
But bulbuls belong in a different bracket.
The pesky bulbul is actually kin
to the melodious nightingale, so when
you hear a whole tree full of evening racket
that hurts people's ears all the way to China,
that's mynah.

BIRD LIGHT

At first I thought my eyes were blurred.
The light went from green to yellow to bird.
Yes, bird. A pigeon had built her nest
in the traffic light. She liked red best.
A perfect place (to a pigeon brain)
to escape from cats and rats and rain.
That bird made an eerie silhouette
when the red went on behind her, and yet
nobody else seemed to notice all day.
Some drivers don't see red lights anyway.

Imagine an officer telling the fellow
who claimed he went all the way through on yellow:
"I believe you fudged that just a smidgen.
You should have come to a stop at the pigeon."

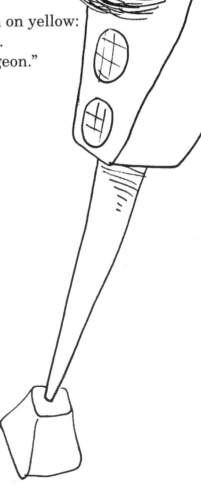

LOOKS

It's true, my right cheek does have a mole.
Were you expecting a Tootsie Roll®?
And yes, those little white things are zits.
And no, my bowlegs don't give me fits.

So what if I'm getting lūʻau feet
from going barefoot down Punchbowl Street?
At least I'll never have corns or bunions
or socks that smell worse than rotten onions.

How come you always point out my flaws,
my ears that don't match and my hands like paws?
Aren't you just trying to distract my view
from the zillions of really weird things about you?

I'd never mention your top-lip fuzz,
your daikon legs, your hair like tar,
or the blue tattoo on your nose, because
to me you're fine the way you are.

PARTY SHOES

After the party—so many shoes!
It's hard to figure out whose are whose
except for Aunt Emily's pink plastic slides
and Robby Boy's black leather double-wides.
There are sandals and high-heels and velcro sneakers,
running shoes, hikers, and rundown squeakers,
and as for the nieces and nephews and cousins,
their Longs rubber slippers spread out by the dozens.

But I have no problem locating my own.
In that jumble of footwear one pair stands alone—
my atomic deep purple Pumas® with white
leather swirls on the sides—they are dynamite!
I'm proud of my Pumas®, I have to admit.
I wriggle them on and I boogie a bit.

Then somebody calls out, "Hey, wait, those are *mine*."
It's Roxanne, whining her usual whine.
"No way," I tell her. "Don't try to be funny.
I paid for these shoes with my very own money."
"YOU GIVE THEM BACK!" She starts in crying.
I sure have to hand it to her for trying,
but what an act! Does she really think
I'd give her my Pumas® and not even blink?

I take my sweet time retying one lace.
Roxanne gets a popped-balloon look on her face.
I sashay and leave her sputtering there.
But walking back home I become aware
that my Pumas® are rubbing me just a touch.
I decide that I must have eaten too much,
so I'd better just put my new shoes away
and not wear them again until Saturday.

I open the closet, and what do you know!
TWO pairs of purple stand toe to toe.
Oh.
Right.
I wore rubber slippers tonight.

MY VERY SHORT 'UKULELE CAREER

I don't even know how to tune this thing.
The other kids all have a song they sing
for tuning, and after several tries
their dogs have fleas. My dog has flies.
Though I practice the chords in the songbook daily,
I'm definitely flunking 'ukulele.

I thought I could learn to strum and pluck,
and in a few weeks with any luck
I'd appear on TV like Jammin' Jake
Shimabukuro. My mistake.
Not only don't I have Jake's cool,
I must have the tinnest ear in school.

Help, Miss Kim Chee! I feel so dumb,
and the May Day program is almost here!
"Try not to hum. Just *pretend* to strum.
Ah, that sounds so much better, dear."

WHAT RAYLEEN'S BROTHER SAID ABOUT A FRESH LOTUS POD SHE BOUGHT AT THE FLORIST SHOP WITH HER ALLOWANCE AND PUT IN A SPECIAL VASE BY THE WINDOW

"You spent good money for that thing? Gee,
it looks like a showerhead to me."

AN ARGUMENT

If we could agree to just disagree
we wouldn't have to fight.
Okay, okay, so you're never wrong,
but that doesn't mean you're right!

SOCCER FOOD SHOULDN'T BE GREEN

Soccer is fun on all days but one,
and that's because of the eats.
Most moms bring us sodas and spam musubi
Or chocolate-chip cookies for treats.

When it's Randall's mom's turn (it's her turn a lot),
she brings yogurty cheese on rye
and other weird things that are good for us (not),
like green kiwi juice that she's juiced on the spot,
or tofu and broccoli pie.

We've prayed for a break, but her latest mistake
almost sent us all to the lua.
Believe it or not, the snack that we got
was boiled-Brussels-sprout manapua.

The team's mad at Randall, but what can he do?
The guy's getting thinner and thinner.
Instead of his mother's watercress stew,
he dreams of spaghetti and pizza, too.
Let's invite him to our house for dinner!

LI HING LOU

Lou Elizabeth Ashley Lui
goes nowhere without her li hing mui,
the powdered kind. It's not only for juices.
She says she's discovered some practical uses.

She carries it in a big glass jar
with pukas on top. "Don't think it's bizarre,"
says Lou. "It makes popcorn 'onolicious,
but it's also perfect for washing dishes."

"It strengthens your immune system, too.
Your tongue may turn red, but you won't get the flu.
Good for what ails you, good for what's scary,
drives away anything germy or hairy."

(You won't find monsters under Lou's bed,
just traces of li hing mui instead).

Lou's mui does magic, or didn't you hear?
She made Kai's report card disappear.
Just a sprinkle and *poof!* his troubles were done.
But Li Hing Lou had only begun.

"That's practice" she told us, acting mysterious,
yet nobody realized she was serious
'til we came to school and found this red pile.
Nothing is left of Lou now but her smile.

There's no need to tell you this any louder.
You guessed it. Lou has taken a powder.

DAYDREAM QUEEN

The teacher says Maile loses more papers
than any student she's seen.
She's late to school and forgets to go home,
so we call her the Daydream Queen.
But I've heard the song she made up about ginger
in bloom by the roadside, and then
I've noticed the drawings she does in her notebook
again and again and again
of the foam on the lip of a tumbling wave
or a rice bird dusting its wing
or the teacher's hands as she reads us a story—
that girl can draw anything.
I'm thinking that maybe our nickname for Maile
is true, but it could be false.
Maybe her mind isn't absent at all,
it's just present somewhere else.

TEACHER'S PET

I know Miss Kim Chee is fond of me
'cause she writes my name on the board
and keeps me with her for hours after school
to go over the math I've ignored.
She was so impressed with the centipede
I brought in for show and tell,
she sent me down to the principal's office
so he could enjoy it as well.
She tells me my science reports are fiction,
my history answers are, too.
"Even your spelling's creative," she says.
"There was never a student like you."
We get our report cards this afternoon.
I hardly can wait, you know.
I've really gone over the top this time—
Miss Kim Chee told me so.
A is for average, B is for better,
but I'm not satisfied
with anything less than F's for fantastic!!!
to fill Miss Kim Chee with pride.
There's a chance I can get into college now
and even earn a degree.
It's a one-in-a-hundred-million chance,
according to Miss Kim Chee.

MILD BOAR

A boar wandered into our class today.
The teacher screamed and jumped on her chair.
We jumped up too, but the boar just lay
like a rug on the floor with his bristly hair

and a wide, tusky grin for Miss Kim Chee.
Not a snort or a grunt came out of his snout.
He gazed at all of us patiently,
especially the teacher, who mellowed out.

"This boar isn't wild, he's mild," she said.
"Please take your seats. He can stay if he's good."
The boar raised his ears while she sat and read
a story, as if he understood.

Miss Kim Chee smiled and said, "Children, look,
he's here to learn, unlike some I could mention.
Will somebody please lend the boar a book?
Such curiosity! Such attention!"

But just as he seemed to catch on to school
and was using his hooves to do his addition,
the boar broke the one unbreakable rule—
he went to the bathroom without permission.

P. U.! Right away the custodian came
and tried to mop up while he held his nose.
The girls all gagged and called out "Shame!"
The boar hung his head and slowly rose,

took a last look around, trotted out through the door.
"I'm awfully sorry he had to go,"
sighed Miss Kim Chee. "Such a curious boar.
What *do* you suppose he wanted to know?"

THE TALLEST GIRL

Most of the boys barely come to her waist.
For the classroom picture, she's always placed
in the back. Sitting down. And still she towers.
(They say she lies down to take her showers).
She's about as tall as a girl can get.
In basketball practice, she holds up the net.
And at Halloween, the costume she chose
was Mauna Loa. Not many of those.
It's a good thing she's nice, or the class would be madder,
'cause to give her stink-eye, you'd need a ladder.

Being that tall has some good points. She
picks coconuts without climbing the tree.
And someone mile-high gets respect, that's for sure.
Even the teachers look up to her.
And yet she wishes her height would drop.
She says it gets lonely at the top.
Miss Kim Chee tells her, *be patient, dear.*
Everyone else will catch up next year.
But for now she makes the whole class look puny,
this giant surrounded by menehune.

CLEANING OUT MY ROOM

"Will you PLEASE get rid of some of this STUFF!"
begged Mom. But it's going to be kind of tough.
I can choose what to toss. It's up to me.
But I don't see junk here. All I see
is a yo-yo stuck on a knotted string,
a pop-top lei, a power ring,
a CD that's only a little bit scratched,
a mynah egg that has never hatched,
a third-prize ribbon, a jar of nails,
my whole collection of gecko tails,
some rusty tweezers, a suitcase key,
bark from the eucalyptus tree,
a Legos® mail-in catalog,
a dog-collar waiting for a dog,
and the very last piece of Halloween candy—
never know when it might come in handy.
How 'bout the half of a boogie board,
the samurai-figure who's lost his sword,
the best horse picture I ever drew,
the longest thumbnail I ever grew,
and the coconut that still might sprout?
There's nothing here I can live without!

AUNTIE'S EEL

When Auntie heard that it's good for a new tree's soul
to bury a cut-up eel in the planting hole,
she did, but the leaves came out all grayish, and plus
they looked a lot more like fins than leaves to us.

One day as she pulled some weeds from under that tree,
something bit into her skin just below the knee.
She swears it was the eel, amazingly reunited.
"Let's dig him up, kids," she said. "Aren't you excited?"

Not me. I'd much rather look at eels in aquaria
than at the one under Auntie's pink plumeria.

DAD'S WAY OF FISHING

He won't say where he's going, or if,
but we follow him out to his favorite cliff.
He doesn't want even the fish to know,
so we whisper. He never did say we could go,

but he's brought enough fishing gear for three.
We figure the simple rule must be:
bring what you need, bait your hook, and wait.
He passes the bucket full of bait.

We cast our lines out and hope for a hit.
Now comes the hard part. We sit. And sit.

Three times we pull up and lose our bite
but Dad lets his fish run out and fight
then brings him in closer with the reel
a turn at a time. He's got the feel.

It's the same at home when we get too rough,
and he lets us go 'til we've had enough.
He's a magnet of calm in all that din—
He just sits there awhile, then he reels us in.

WHAT'S IN A NAME?

Some animals' names make them she's or he's,
like DAMSELflies or MANatees.
The Hawaiian monk seal sounds like a mister,
but shouldn't he have a nun seal sister?
Some ladybugs really are boy bugs you know,
and for every tilapia … a tilapio.
It's a cowfrog the bullfrog is bellowing for,
and there have to be Portuguese Women-of-war
or they'd all be finished by this time next spring.
Those spooky blue jellies would go … ex-sting!

SHARING A TWINKIE® IN THE VALLEY

Jake hiked all morning with his friend Camille
then they plopped down, tired, for their noontime meal.
That day almost ruined their spring vacation,
beginning with lunchtime conversation.
Camille said, "Why don't we share our food,
including dessert?" Jake's answer was rude.

"You mean half my Twinkie® for half your plum?
I guess you must think I'm pretty dumb.
If you like Twinkies®, then bring your own.
I'm eating this puppy all alone."
"What a PIG you are, Jake Salvador.
"I'm not going hiking with you anymore."

Then something came huffing down the trail.
A dog. But he wasn't wagging his tail
or anything else. He stopped and leered
at their food. Then two other dogs appeared.
They were mean-looking poi-dogs, drooly and bony,
and what they wanted was Jake's baloney.

Now Jake had always been just a little
afraid of dogs with big teeth and spittle.
"Let's give them some of our sandwich," he said,
so each of them pulled off a crust of bread
and tossed it to the dogs who gulped it down
then waited for more. One seemed to frown

and growled. Jake threw the entire thing.
Camille tossed her tuna. The dogs formed a ring.
Camille yelled, "The Twinkie®! Tear it in three!"
Jake told his dessert, "Better you than me,"
and moaned as the dogs wolfed down the cake.
Now they had nothing to eat but Jake.

"The plum! Throw the plum, Camille! That's it!"
One swallowed it whole, including the pit.
There was no more food. Jake looked at his friend.
The dogs moved closer. So this was the end.

Maaaaiiiiii! The dogs pricked up their ears.
Then a hunter strolled up, and eased Jake's fears.
"Silly mutts," said the man. "Whatcha tryin' to do?
Hey kids, did these monsters bother you?
Beg for your food or scare you? I'm sorry.
With these dogs of mine, there's no need to worry.

"They run pretty good and they're kind of big,
but they're not going to hurt anyone but a pig."
The dogs obeyed his command to heel.
A pig? whispered Jake. He leaned on Camille.

As soon as the man and his dog-pack were gone,
Jake turned to Camille and swore, "from now on
I'm sharing with you like you share with me.
A pig is the last thing I want to be."

33

SHARK ADVICE

If you paddle alone into murky water,
you'll look like a dolphin more that you oughter.
A shark craves dolphins but isn't too bright,
so he sinks his teeth in whatever looks right.
We taste bad to sharks, so they bite us and spit.
But if you are the bitten, one bite could be IT.
This beast likes his teething toys raw and steamy
so unless you'd like to be kid-sashimi
forget about swimming too close to dark.
It's a bad idea to confuse a shark.

SHARKS, TOO

Though people think sharks who bite people are worse,
more people eat sharks than the reverse.
Shark parents all warn their sons and daughters,
"No swimming in shark-ingested waters!

CHARLENE'S FIRST WAVE

Charlene couldn't let one more wave get away
and leave her behind, so she tried to hurry.
An old waterman who rode one wave a day
told her "Waves take time. There's time, no worry."

She lay on her longboard and closed her eyes,
allowing herself to just bob and drift.
Through the board she could feel the deep water rise,
the back of her surfboard beginning to lift,

then something inside her, but not in her mind,
a humming somewhere in her body said NOW!
She paddled hard 'til she thought she could find
her balance, then stood up and stayed on somehow

to join with the water moving below.
Stood up on the ocean, alone and free,
Charlene and the wave. It seemed as though
there was no other world, no Waikīkī,

just plenty of time! The old man was right.
There was only one wave, and its crest shone bright.

THE HONU'S SECRETS

Experts can tell us without much doubt
if a boy or a girl turtle's going to come out

of the egg. They say it depends on the weather
(if it's cool, it's a boy). They can tell you whether

it's a green sea turtle or some other kind.
They know there is one big thing on his mind:

how fast he must scurry across the sand
to escape grave danger. They understand

the hunger of ghost crabs who lie in wait.
The turtle experts can calculate

precisely the odds that he will survive
and get to the water's edge alive.

But where it is that he goes when he goes
and exactly how old he grows when he grows

nobody knows.

LIMOUSINE MYSTERIES

Kids, ever watch a limo go by
(and by and by and by) and try
to peek in through the tinted glass
to see who is traveling first class?

Who's seeing the island without being seen?
The lieutenant governor? The queen?
Is it TV stars, or maybe a harem?
Do they have seatbelts, and do they wear 'em?

A LIMOUSINE DRIVER TELLS ALL

I'll tell you who *I* drive every day.
They're tourists. A lot like us, I've found,
but richer, with lots more time to play.
Except they *don't* play, they just ride around
saying, "When do we get to Kapolei?"

Driving a limo? It could be worse.
Some drivers end up having to drive
the dead for a living in a long, black hearse.
At least my clients are still alive.

Though you'd think a chauffeur might be a snob,
you never will hear me brag or boast.
This is just another demanding job.
A limo is harder to steer than a post.

But I can't complain. I like getting paid.
If life hands you limos, make limo-nade!

SKATEBOARD HERO

Seth jumped on his board and went down to the mall.
There's a skate ramp and rail there, but that's about all.
Seth's good at skateboarding. Really good.
From the time he was five, he understood
that you have to take risks if you want to learn.
Sometimes you crash, and sometimes you burn.
But it's worse to play safe and not even try,
so he got lots of bruises and one black eye,
and now he is eight and can skate. No doubt!
But some big guys were checking the mall ramp out.

Seth knew what was coming, he was used to the jeers.
Hey kid, come back in about ten years.
He hung back and watched them do their stuff.
Their flip-outs were good, but they weren't good enough.
As soon as they stopped to catch a breath
and swallow some soda, up rolled Seth,
did a one-wheel 360 and climbed the rail
for a one-hand handstand. They thought he would bail,
but he backslapped out, rolling smooth and flat.
Where'd a kid like you learn to skate like that?
"Right here," said Seth. *For real?* said the guy.
You should get you a sponsor. You wanna try?
I bet my uncle could find you one.
"No thanks," said Seth, "I just skate for fun."

They leaned on their boards to watch his shuvit
and impossible wheelie. They had to love it.
He nailed one-wheel manual and Chinatown,
but the guys had to leave when the sun went down.
So long, dude, maybe we'll see you later.
Keep that up, you're the Terminator!

Seth may be young and short and small
but they don't call him little.
Not at the mall.

THE LOST ART OF FLYING

Sam flaps his arms, but he soon gives up trying
because he is seven now.
Young enough to remember flying.
Too old to remember how.

CAT MAGNET

I'm not a cat-person, I never was,
but cats don't seem to know that because,
though I sit on the sofa and fold my hands,
and tuck my feet under and make no demands,
while other kids call out "Here, kitty, here, cat,"
the darn thing will run to me just like that,
jump into my lap and nuzzle my chin.
It meows at me until I give in
and scratch it a little under its ruff,
then meows when I stop. It can't get enough.
Even its owner can't tell me why.
"I don't understand. She's usually shy."

There *are* some cats I think I could like
who live at the park where I ride my bike.
They hide in the bushes, I don't know how many.
When I offer them food, they won't eat any
'til after I'm gone. One's kind of gray.
No one bothers him, and he likes to play
with the red-grass tips. He leaves the nest
and comes out more often than the rest.
He suns in the open, but keeps his distance,
raising one paw to note my existence
(or is he only scratching a flea?).
I wish that cat would come to me.

THE WALLABY

I thought I saw a wallaby.
No, no, I did see a wallaby.
It's everyone else who only thought
I imagined I saw it.
Here, I'll draw it.

It had little dog-like ears and head.
"Then it *was* a dog," my mother said.
But a dog wouldn't have this wallaby tail
that thumped behind him down the trail.
Kai said he bet that was just a root,
but a root wouldn't move. A root, my foot!

I really did see it, so why didn't they
turn and look before it hopped away?
"It's a legend," said Dad, "and shouldn't you wonder
how a wallaby got here from far Down Under?"
It's obvious they don't believe.
They tell me I'm much too naive.

I wish I could draw the thoughts I think
about life in the mountains with rain to drink.
A wallaby life where wild ginger blooms.
A secret life. A life without rooms.

You know, my wild little wallaby ought
to stay in the shadows and never get caught
or the whole town will see him. In the zoo.
So why don't we keep this just between you
and me? I did see a wallaby.

WELL, SHE ASKED

Mom opens her magazine and yawns.
So how was school today?
She glances up, then back at the page.
There's not much to tell, I say.

You'll see us tonight on the local news—
some guy who was short and handsome
tried to take over the 8 o'clock bus
and hold us kids for ransom.

But we yelled like crazy and threw our slippers
and beaned him with our lunch,
so he dived for the door and ran for his life
to escape such a rowdy bunch.

Mr. Wong had a substitute today
who taught us to play gin rummy,
then right after five-draw poker I felt
a sharp pain in my tummy.

"Appendicitis," the school nurse said.
But you don't have to worry—
she treated me with a heaping plate
of Indonesian curry.

The afternoon moved kind of slow
except for one surprise.
They announced the spelling bee results
and awarded me grand prize:

a king-sized Harley-Davidson
with tons of shiny chrome-work.
I drove it home all by myself.

That's nice, dear. Any homework?

FIELD TRIP OF DREAMS

"Can you think of a perfect excursion, class,
both educational and fun?"
Sure, Miss Kim Chee, so glad you asked.
We can come up with lots more than one.

Instead of attending a kiddie show
where we'll squirm and twiddle our thumbs,
let's all go to Kenny Endo's place
and beat on his taiko drums.

Let's spend all afternoon in a hot air balloon,
that's something we've never tried.
Or skateboard right through a lava tube
and come out on the other side.

Sign us up for a day of karate—
we just love that growling noise.
To make this a learning experience,
the girls get to throw the boys.

Here's how to make a trip to the zoo
more fun than it's been for ages:
have us pretend we're the hairy apes
and climb right into their cages.

Bicycle safety courses are lame,
with both hands on the handlebars.
So how 'bout a class at Raceway Park
where they let us kids drive the cars?

Next time it's time to demolish a building,
take us down to the site on the bus.
Someone must push that blaster button,
so why shouldn't it be us?

If that's impossible, here's a sure-fire
winner, you will see:
a session of hands-on make-and-take
at the fireworks factory.

Say yes to one of these trips, Miss Kim Chee,
and we're sure it will come to pass:
on excursion day every kid in the world
will beg to be in your class.

KYLE'S QUESTIONS

Kyle seldom asks questions, but when he does,
we look up and hold our breath, because
we know he won't ask what page we're on,
or where all the blackboard chalk has gone.

Kyle's questions can throw us into reverse,
like: *what lies beyond the universe?*
or: *there's too many wars, so what's the deal?*
or: *if dogs see different from us, what's real?*

Why didn't we think of that? Our eyes
are on Miss Kim Chee, who simply sighs
and says, "Fine questions, but I'm afraid
to answer would take 'til eleventh grade."

Dust particles surf on a ray of light
while we think about stars, or wars, or sight.
Then it's time for things we *can* learn this year,
like math and how to spell atmosphere.

CONNECTING WITH BECKY

Becky has all the latest gear.
Everything's beeping, a plug in each ear.
Her player's digital, her notebook's solar.
There's a tiny telephone in her molar.

She'll go to the beach, but she can't get wet
or she might lose her line to the Internet.
When you see her shopping at Ala Moana
or attending a lūʻau with her ʻohana,
she's always on-line, ignoring the scene.
She might as well be in quarantine.

Want to talk to her? You will have to dial.
Though she's standing next to you all the while,
don't expect to get through without some luck.
She'll only pick up if her cursor's stuck.
She's so busy sending, there's no time at all
for the tinkling chime of an incoming call.

We feel like our friend has disappeared.
She's wired and wireless and weird.
She used to be real. Won't somebody please
disconnect all those batteries?

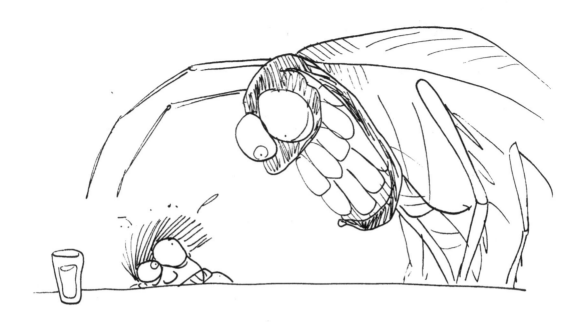

MY BROTHER AND THE ROACH

He swallowed a roach when he was one.
It fell in his milk, and he drank it down.

By the time he was four, he gagged and turned pale
when we brought up that old roach-swallowing tale.

If we whispered "roach" when he was eight,
He pushed away both his milk and his plate.

At ten, he eats nothing that milk might touch
"because of the pesticides and such."
(Wouldn't pesticides mean no more roach?)

My little brother was a heck of a lot more fun
when he was one.

MONA AND THE WHALE

Mona's friends weren't exactly slim,
but they called her Momona, meaning fat.
Yes, she was heavy, but she could swim.
In the water, she was an acrobat.

They did some snorkeling close to shore.
When Mona surfaced, she gave a shout,
"Look! Out there! I see three! I see four!
Some humpback whales had begun to spout.

Then one heaved up like a submarine rising.
Up out of the water rose all that weight
in a powerful arc that was so surprising
Mona smiled to herself. That whale looked great!

With its flippers folded, effortless,
the whale splashed down. Then somebody said,
"Momona, that's you," and Mona thought *Yes*
as the whales swam off toward Koko Head.

Yes, I'm a whale, and she felt at peace
to be something that beautiful in motion.
No one would call a whale obese.
I am an Amazon of the ocean.

BON DANCE

All year long I never can please
my mom, as though I have some disease
called "not quite right" or "could be better."
I follow instructions to the letter
for folding the laundry or shelving books,
but she just gives me those so-so looks.
I can't wrap a package or tie the bow,
and I'm perfectly hopeless trying to sew.
I swear she frowns at my every movement.
She says, *There's always room for improvement.*

At last comes another o-bon season.
Mom always starts out by explaining the reason:
we dance under lanterns and make a feast
to welcome back family who are deceased.
It's important to do everything just right …
But something comes over us both that night
as we put on yukata and tie up our hair
and mumble our ancestor-honoring prayer.

We're off to the dance at the hongwanji
and Mom hasn't said one word to me
about how to behave, so I hold her hand
as we cross the grounds by the meat stick stand.
You look like Aunt Miko, Mom says with a tear
(she said the exact same thing last year).

We join with her friends, dancing side by side,
and circle the tower. With Mom as my guide
I remember the steps, and she nods to me.
Together we clap and turn beautifully.

No room for improvement! It's marvelous—
I'm not a "you" to her now, I'm an "us."
I'm more than a girl, Mom's more than a mother.
We move to the drumbeat and smile at each other,
forgetting our could-be-better routine
at o-bon time, the time in-between.

THE INVISIBLE STING

Box jellies are clear as cellophane.
The less you see, the more the pain.

THAT'LL SHOW 'EM

A sea cucumber, when he wants to pout,
turns his entire self inside out.
If you've ever seen this, you may deplore it,
but sea cucumbers have the stomach for it.

ONE FRIEND AND ANOTHER

When I'm with Lisa, I don't seem to matter.
My dreams, like pebbles underwater,
are colorful, so perfect to share,
but they dry to gray when exposed to her air.

When I'm with Alana, my dreams unfold
like bird-of-paradise, orange and gold
with a spear of blue. Her laughter's the rain
that washes all Lisa-thoughts from my brain
so I don't believe I'm an ignoramus.
With Alana I'm brilliant and funny and famous.

THANK YOU NOTES

My birthday's over, and I'm stuck at the table.
I'd rather be mucking out the stable
or pedaling my bike through a mile of sand
than writing out thank-you notes by hand.
This card has "Mahalo" printed right on it.
I don't know why I couldn't just sign it.
Impersonal, Mom says. *That wouldn't do.*
They went to some trouble, and so can you.
Just a few little words. Your arm won't break.
The trouble is, everything sounds so fake.
I can't say **Dear Auntie, that shirt you made**
would be perfect for someone in second grade,
or **I'm so, so glad you got me another**
Goodnight Gecko. I'll give it to brother.

There must be some way I can be polite
but say what I mean and mean what I write.
I really don't know how to thank you, Aunt Mo.
How true! So that's one down, and one to go.
Now Gramma. Oh dear. I really do like
the headlight she got for me for my bike
and all the great things she does for me.
I love to go see her in Kaimukī.
She calls from the porch when she sees me coming
then squeezes me hard and starts in humming
that song, "Sweet Someone." I love her hands.
I love how she always understands
and laughs her big laugh with one tooth missing.
With Gramma I even put up with kissing.
Are there words for that? I have to try.
Dear Gramma, I hope you never die.

MY SUMMER PLANS

No hot soccer clinics or summer school.
I'm not even tempted to go to the pool.
I'll sleep until noon in my bed full of crumbs.
For exercise maybe I'll wiggle my thumbs.

I'll chew wads of gum and blow a big bubble
unless even that seems like too much trouble.
I'll bathe if I want to and not, if not.
When it comes to tooth brushing, my molars can rot.

Don't make appointments and don't point to clocks.
I won't put on underwear, sneakers, or socks.
If I lie without moving for weeks in the grass,
just mow right around me and fill up my glass.

I'll keep my eyes closed so I don't get too dizzy
from watching while everyone else keeps busy.
Call me a slug, say I'm sure to grow dumber,
but remember, I'm doing nothing all summer.

NOW OR NEVER

The day Mr. Lee turned a hundred and three
he knew he was getting old.
Yet he wondered about, couldn't quite figure out,
how to live the way he'd been told.

Should he stay where he was or travel around?
Live in Kaimukī or Rome?
It's true *a rolling stone gathers no moss,*
but *there's no place* quite *like home.*

Should he go for it, trying everything out,
or be cautious like the rest?
Better be safe than sorry, they say,
and *experience teaches best.*
Silence is golden, and yet we're told
the squeaky wheel gets the grease.
Should he keep his achievements to himself,
or send out a press release?

All things come to those who wait,
but *there's no time like the present.*
Which of these was the best advice?
The answer might not be pleasant.

All of his life he's never made waste
by doing a single thing in haste,
but when he dies he'll be double-crossed—
because *he who hesitates is lost.*

Will absence make our hearts grow fonder
Of Mr. Lee and his kind?
Or will this be just another case
of *out of sight, out of mind*?

AT HOME WITH MRS. GOMES

Mrs. Gomes is different, and here's the proof:
she lives in a house that has no roof.
When Hurricane Ed blew it off last year
and her son came to fix it, she said, "thanks, dear,
but I've lived my whole life with a lid on, you see.
I think I will try just the sky and me."

Her stay-at-home evenings are never dull.
She reads on the couch when the moon is full
or keeps a lookout for shooting stars.
She can pick out the Pleiades now, and Mars.
Even by day she may stay in bed
enjoying the cloud show overhead.
To her it's the wonder of Kahaluʻu—
not only a room, a whole house with a view!

On cleaning day, she opens her doors
and allows the trade winds to sweep her floors.
When it rains, she showers and washes her clothes
and waters her fern and her tuberose.
The few things she needs, she keeps in a chest
where they won't get wet. She got rid of the rest.

People who live in weatherproof homes
can't imagine the freedom of Mrs. Gomes.
In fact, just last week someone heard her say,
"I'm thinking of giving my walls away."

IN THE FUTURE

I try to imagine my life in the future:
I see myself driving. I'm finally tall.
I'm having no trouble whistling at all,
but I must have a job, so what will I do?
Will I doze in an office? muck out at the zoo?
fly a helicopter or write a book?
be a volleyball coach or a sushi cook?

Will I still like to skate? Will I still have fun?
Will I still be me when I'm twenty-one?

INDEX